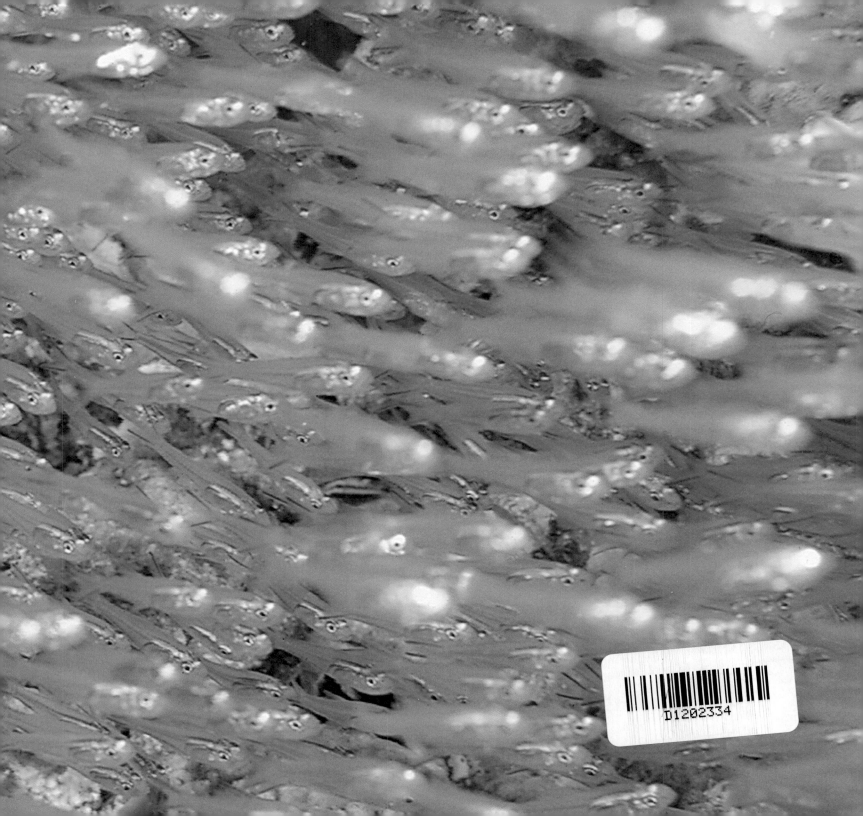

a slice of port douglas

Project Manager/Editor: Debbie Haydock
Writer: Lisa McLeod
Art Director: Gretta Kool
Photographer: Ross Isaacs
– Ocean Planet Images
Food Photographer: Ken Middleton
Additional Photography: Stephen Nutt
Consultant Chef: Mick Webb
Copy Editor: Sir Kenneth Trezise OBE
Scanning, Pre-press & Printing:
Fergies Printing Pty Ltd,
37 College Street, Hamilton, Qld 4007
Australia

ISBN: 0-9581687-0-9

Bound in Melbourne, Australia

Available through Debbie Haydock
PO Box 519, Port Douglas Queensland
4871 Australia
Tel: 0438 409931
Fax: + (61 7) 4099 4569
Email: debbiehaydock@ledanet.com.au
www.asliceofportdouglas.com.au

Published by Vicki & Byron Kurth and
Debbie Haydock

Cataloguing-in-Publication

A Slice of Port Douglas

Includes index

Cookery – Queensland – Port Douglas

acknowledgements

Writing the acknowledgements for everyone who has contributed to the success of *A Slice of Port Douglas* is a difficult task. Many people from the Port Douglas community have shared their love, support, friendship and encouragement to help me fulfil my dream of producing this book. For this I am grateful.

I could not have succeeded without the love of my sons – William and Jake and my Mum Jenny, all of whom have continually supported me in my endeavors. They always offered an ear to listen, a voice to ground me, and love to encourage me.

Vicki and Byron Kurth, my publishers believed in this book and deserve the biggest thanks – it won't be the last they see of me! Thank you to Ross Isaacs' sensational photography and blind faith in my abilities. Lisa McLeod who conjured the words to flow through the images. Gretta Kool for showing me perfectionism and visual beauty. Ken Middleton, who I know glides on water when thrown in deep.

A special thanks to Mick Webb who worked long hours sacrificing many weekend jaunts to help style the food and recipes with expertise. Vera Falovic, a special friend who always listened and supported me.

To the Chefs, Restaurateurs and their staff who provided exquisite recipes – thank you for your commitment and support.

Finally, this book would not have been possible without the following contributors:

Myer Grace Bros	Wavelength
House Stuff (Cairns)	CJ Fischer
Rainforest Habitat	Phillip Martin
Judy Gittings	Stephen Nutt
Alan & Susan Carle	Steve Brennan
Botanical Ark	Whyanbeel Arboretum
Excel Trading	Margaret Everett
Steve Broomhall	Terry Hooper & staff
Rachael Haydon &	Jungle Bookshop
Meagan Hepworth	Wally & Maureen Gray

a slice of port douglas

contents

1 ▶ intro

Port Douglas is an open window on the world, through which blows a constant stream of new elements

In recent years the village of Port Douglas, situated on a tiny isthmus on the far northeastern coast of Australia, has grown rapidly in popularity and is now one of the world's most well-known tourist destinations.

Port Douglas is perfectly positioned as a starting point for journeys to the region's natural attractions. Reef… rainforest… outback… and beaches, with Port Douglas at the epicentre. On the one hand, it's a village where everything lies within walking distance. On the other hand, you're just as likely to rub shoulders with Mick Jagger strolling through the Marina; Sean Penn sipping café lattes; or Bill Clinton leaning in the doorway of a hotel, enjoying some Irish music and soaking up that inimitable Port Douglas ambience.

Perhaps one of the most likeable elements contributing to Port Douglas's atmosphere is the unhurried manner, the genuine feeling of welcome that you come across. The lack of pretension sets it apart from other destinations. It's unhip and happy… laid-back but not falling over. The Port Douglas area offers a diversity of eco-systems and landscapes paralleled by the smorgasbord of experiences on offer.

It's a microcosm reflecting Australia's emerging style, paying homage to the area's melting pot of culinary influences and placing them in its modern Asian context.

Port Douglas is an open window on the world, through which blows a constant stream of new

It's a microcosm reflecting Australia's emerging style, paying homage to the area's melting pot of culinary influences

Above left: Cooper Creek. Above right: Wine & Food Festival, Carnivale. Opposite: Four Mile Beach.

Port Douglas offers a diversity of eco-systems and landscapes paralleled by the smorgasboard of experiences on offer

elements. Without the millennia of established traditions to respect or preserve, there's always room for new influences.

Since the late 19th century – when one of Port Douglas's first tourists wrote an account of being unceremoniously dumped into a dinghy with the baggage, left to clamber onto the wharf and stumble off into the dark, tripping over goats in the search for board and lodging – the town has gathered somewhat more to offer in terms of dining and accommodation choices. These days the gastronomic adventure itself is often one of the most memorable elements of a holiday in Port Douglas. Working with the abundance of fresh seafood at their doorstep and a treasure trove of exotic ingredients to draw from and experiment with, over the years Port Douglas chefs have been able to re-interpret such diverse cuisines as Mediterranean and Pacific Islander.

By the 1950's, when the Bowdens opened the legendary *Nautilus Restaurant*, the name Port Douglas had become synonymous with good food.

These days Port Douglas offers such a variety of dining experiences that you'll be spoilt for choice. Don't worry if you don't get a chance to experience all the options – you can always recreate those taste sensations in the comfort of your own home. Just take this definitive collection of recipes with you, turn up the central heating, pull out the sarong, stick an umbrella in your drink – then sit back and dream on!

Right: one of the many spectacular views of the coastal road leading into Port Douglas. Above right: Aerial of Port Douglas, photograph by Stephen Nutt.

2 ▸ calm

Sun is gentle... soft sand melts beneath your feet like warm talcum powder

Horizon and
sky are a
seamless
vision of
tranquil pale
blue water

Wake at daybreak to drink in the peace, the vast expanse of pale blue water. Horizon and sky are a seamless vision of tranquillity. Soft sand melts beneath your feet like warmed talcum powder. Air, water and skin… one shared temperature. Float on its surface, warm and safe; the air is still, sun is gentle this early in the morning. The whole sky belongs only to you.

The white sands of Four Mile Beach lie before you. Why not beachcomb your way to breakfast? A clear stretch of she-oak and coconut palms line the beach's edge. Half an hour of tropical beauty before you reach the cafes of Macrossan Street. A good dose of space to clear the head and refresh the spirit.

Maybe it's time to sleep in, then café crawl your way down to breakfast and a family day on the beach. Pull up some shade and chill out as that warm breeze slides through the palm fronds overhead. Tuck a frangipani blossom behind your ear to add the finishing touch to the most perfectly clear blue sunshiney day.

Clockwise from top: Double Island; Four Mile Beach; room service with a view; beachcomb your way to breakfast.
Opposite: white sails pass through the inlet into the big blue.

13

The vast expanse... a good
dose of space to clear the
head and refresh the spirit

Left: sailing the vast expanse. Below: Four Mile Beach against a backdrop of distant mountain peaks. Opposite, clockwise from right: warm breeze slides through palm fronds overhead; Bougainvillea flower; sun is gentle this early in the morning. Previous page: wake at daybreak to drink in the peace with an early morning walk on Four Mile Beach.

Wake at daybreak. Air, water and skin... one shared temperature

Clockwise from top:
day breaks at Four
Mile Beach; life-
guard surveying the
scene; the sun sets
on Four Mile Beach;
rigours of another
day in paradise.
Opposite: fishing on
Four Mile Beach.

Grilled prawn skewers

with lemon myrtle and mango dressing and jasmine rice pilaf

Serves 4

ingredients

16 leader prawns or large tiger prawns
4 leaves of fresh lemon myrtle or kaffir lime leaves, julienned
1 lemon, zested and juiced
1 tsp black pepper, freshly cracked
100mls vegetable oil

lemon myrtle & mango dressing
4 mango cheeks, fresh or frozen (prefer just under ripe)
1 tbsp lemon myrtle oil
2 tbsps virgin olive oil
1 tbsp lemon juice (omit if mango not ripe)

jasmine rice pilaf
1 onion, finely chopped
2 cloves garlic, finely chopped
1 tbsp oil
1 cup jasmine rice
2 cups water or good-quality fish stock
salt & pepper, to taste

Peel prawns, leaving heads and tails intact then thread onto skewers. Combine lemon myrtle, lemon zest and juice, pepper and oil and pour over prawns. Refrigerate and marinate for at least 2 hours.

To make the dressing, place mango, lemon myrtle oil, olive oil and lemon juice (optional) in a food processor and pulse until mixture has a thick consistency.

To make the pilaf, place onion, garlic and oil in a baking tray and cook over a medium heat until onion is soft. Add rice and continue to stir allowing the heat to evenly disperse. Add the water then bring to the boil. Cover with aluminium foil then place tray in a preheated oven at 200ºC for 20 minutes or until the rice is cooked. Remove foil and season with salt and pepper then run fork through the rice so it does not become gluggy.

Remove the prawns from the marinade and cook on a hot chargrill or barbecue for approximately 1 minute each side or until the prawns are cooked.

To serve, place prawns on a serving plate with the rice and dressing. The dressing maybe either drizzled over the prawns or be served as a side dish for dipping.

Twice cooked tuna

Serves 4

ingredients

4 x 200g tuna
4 stalks lemon grass
2 x 4 cm (1½ inch) ginger
2 x 4 cm (1½ inch) galangal
8 cloves of garlic
12 golden shallots
1 litre chicken or fish stock
1 tbsp palm sugar or brown sugar
3 tbsps tamarind jam
2 tbsps fish sauce
1 tbsp oyster sauce
2 long red chillis, seeds removed & halved
Thai red pawpaw, cut into cubes of approx 3 x 3 cm
200g baby spinach

Place lemon grass, ginger, galangal, garlic, shallots and stock into a saucepan and simmer until garlic softens. Add palm sugar, tamarind jam, fish sauce and oyster sauce and continue to simmer for 2 minutes. Remove from heat and infuse for 1 hour. Remove the galangal and ginger. Return saucepan to stove and add chilli and pawpaw. Simmer until pawpaw is soft. Add spinach.

Heat oil in frypan. Gently add tuna and cook for a few seconds on all sides then poach in the broth to your liking – rare is best. Serve in individual bowls immediately. You can add a stalk of lemon grass, half a chilli and fresh coriander for presentation.

Barramundi wings

with brandy mustard sauce

Serves 4

ingredients

12 medium Barramundi wings
2 tbsps garlic butter (softened)
¼ cup chopped mixed herbs
(i.e. dill, parsley & thyme)
1 sweet potato, cut into thin
strips with a peeler
oil, for deep frying
sea salt

brandy mustard sauce

1 tbsp oil
¼ cup spring onions, chopped
¼ cup brandy
½ cup Riesling white wine
1 tbsp grained mustard
1 cup cream
1 tbsp chopped dill

Scale and clean the Barramundi Wings. Place the wings on a greased baking tray with skin side up. Brush with the garlic butter and sprinkle with the herbs. Bake in preheated oven of 200°C for 10-15 minutes or until cooked.

To make the sauce, heat oil in a saucepan and add the spring onions and cook over a medium heat for approximately 1 minute. Add the brandy and wine and bring to the boil. Reduce heat and simmer until the liquid is reduced by half. Add the mustard and cream and simmer for a further 5 minutes or until the sauce thickens. Remove the pan from the heat and add the dill.

Deep fry sweet potato strips in oil over a high heat until golden brown and crisp. Drain on absorbent paper. Sprinkle with sea salt to retain crispness.

Place wings on serving plates, top with sauce and serve with the sweet potato chips.

CHEF'S TIP: You can also use other fish wings e.g. Red Emperor or Coral Trout.

Meze

caprese ı marinated
artichoke hearts ı
kalamata olives &
fetta cheese ı roasted
capsicum & eggplant
roulade ı roasted
mediterranean
vegetables ı
seafood frittata ı
mushroom &
leek tart ı

caprese

4 pieces bocconcini cheese, sliced
3 roma tomatoes, sliced
balsamic vinegar
2 tbsps basil, julienned
cracked black pepper

Arrange a layer of the cheese in a circular pattern alternating with a slice of tomato. Drizzle with the balsamic vinegar, sprinkle the basil over the top and season with the cracked black pepper.

marinated artichoke hearts

4 artichokes, halved
1 tbsp basil, finely chopped
1 tbsp thyme, finely chopped
1 tbsp Italian parsley, finely chopped
½ cup white vinegar
½ cup olive oil
salt & pepper, to taste

Combine all the ingredients and marinate for at least 12 hours.

kalamata olives & fetta cheese

250g pitted kalamata olives
250g fetta cheese, chopped
1 tbsp basil, finely chopped
1 tbsp thyme, finely chopped
1 tbsp Italian parsley, finely chopped
1-2 garlic cloves, crushed
¼ cup olive oil

Combine all ingredients.

roasted capsicum & eggplant roulade

4 red capsicums
1 tbsp olive oil
1 large eggplant, sliced thinly
½ bunch basil leaves, julienned
150g marscarpone cheese
cracked black pepper

Place whole capsicums on a tray under a hot grill. Cook, turning occasionally, until the skin starts to blacken. Place the capsicums in a bowl covered with plastic wrap. When cool, remove the skins. Cut the capsicums in half and remove the seeds. Brush eggplant with oil and then cook on a hot chargrill on both sides until tender. Place a layer of capsicum on a sushi mat then a layer of eggplant, spread with marscarpone then sprinkle with basil and season with pepper then roll. Place the roll in plastic wrap and tighten by twisting the ends. Refrigerate and when set, cut into portions.

roasted mediterranean vegetables

2 tbsps olive oil
1 red capsicum, chopped
1 onion, chopped
1 eggplant, chopped
1 zucchini, chopped
2 cloves garlic, finely chopped
1 tbsp rosemary, finely chopped
1 tbsp thyme, finely chopped
1 tbsp basil, finely chopped
¼ cup balsamic vinegar

Heat oil in a baking tray and when at smoking point, add capsicum, onion, eggplant, zucchini, garlic, rosemary, thyme and basil and cook for 30 seconds without browning. Place vegetables in a preheated oven of 200°C and cook until el dente. Remove the vegetables from the oven and add the vinegar and mix well to combine. Refrigerate and marinate for at least 4 hours.

seafood frittata

5 eggs
¼ cup chives, finely chopped
salt & pepper
1 tbsp oil
½ onion, finely chopped
1 garlic clove, crushed
50g white fish, chopped
25g prawn meat, chopped
25g calamari rings

Place eggs and chives in a large bowl and whisk to combine. Season with salt and pepper. Heat the oil in a frypan. Add onion and garlic and sauté until soft. Add fish, prawn meat and calamari and cook over a medium heat for 2-3 minutes or until not quite cooked. Pour the egg mixture evenly over seafood in frypan and cook over a medium heat for approximately 5 minutes or until it is fully set. Set aside and allow to cool.

mushroom & leek tart

1 tbsp oil
1 leek, thinly sliced
500g button mushroom, sliced
1 tbsp chopped thyme
2 cloves crushed fresh garlic
1 cup shaved parmesan cheese
salt & pepper

pastry

200g plain flour
100g butter
1 egg
1 tbsp thyme, finely chopped
1 tbsp water, approximately

Place flour and butter in a food processor and pulse until mixture resembles fine breadcrumbs. Add egg, thyme and water and mix to a firm dough, adding a little more water, if necessary. Turn out onto a floured surface and knead lightly for 2 minutes. Wrap in plastic wrap and refrigerate for 30 minutes. Roll pastry onto a floured surface to fit a 20cm (8 inch) pie plate. Prick tart with a fork and place a piece of wax paper or aluminium foil in the pastry shell. Fill shell with dried beans or rice. Bake in oven of 180°C for approximately 10 minutes. Remove the weights and paper and bake for a further 3-5 minutes or until pastry is golden brown.

Heat oil in a frypan and add leeks and cook over a medium heat until golden brown. Add mushrooms, thyme and garlic and cook for a further 2 minutes. Strain the mixture to eliminate any excess moisture. Spoon mixture into pastry case and top with parmesan cheese then bake in a preheated oven of 180°C or until cheese becomes golden brown.

Sandcrab & avocado

panna cotta
with margarita
ocean trout
gravalax served
with an oyster
in a wasabi
and rice wine
viniagrette

Serves 4

ingredients

panna cotta
230mls full cream
2 star anise
⅓ cinnamon quill
4 cardamon pods
2 tsps gelatine
2 tbsps water
250g sand crab, cooked and chopped
2 avocados
1 tsp lime juice
1 tbsp fresh coriander, finely chopped
salt and pepper, to taste

margarita gravalax
2 tbsps lime juice
¼ cup coriander, chopped
1 shot Tequila
½ cup sugar
½ cup rock salt
200g ocean trout or atlantic salmon

wasabi & rice wine vinaigrette
2 tbsps wasabi paste
¼ cup rice wine vinegar
½ cup QP mayonnaise
1 tbsp ponzu citrus soy
hondashi powder, to taste
4 fresh oysters in half shell

To prepare the gravalax, combine the lime juice, coriander and Tequila and rub into fish. Combine the sugar and rock salt and completely cover the fish. Refrigerate for at least 24 hours. Wash off salt and sugar, pat dry and slice thinly.

To make the Panna cotta, place cream, star anise, cinnamon and cardamon pods into a saucepan and bring to the boil. Remove from heat to infuse flavours for 15 minutes. Strain. Dissolve gelatine in water and stir into cream mixture. Place avocado, crab, lime juice, coriander, salt and pepper into a blender and process until smooth. Add crab mixture to cream mixture and mix well to combine. Pour mixture into 4 x 1 cup capacity moulds or ramekins and refrigerate for 4 to 5 hours or until firm.

To make the vinaigrette, place the wasabi paste, vinegar, mayonnaise, soy sauce in a blender and process until smooth. Season with hondashi for taste. Pour a little of the dressing into each oyster shell.

To serve, place the Panna cotta on a plate with the ocean trout and the oyster shell.

CHEF'S TIP: All the ingredients in the wasabi and rice wine vinaigrette are available at most asian food stores.

Flaming vodka fettuccini

with scallops and leek in a saffron cream sauce

Serves 4

ingredients

1 cup good-quality dry white wine
¼ tsp saffron strands
½ tsp cracked black pepper
2 cups thickened cream
500g fresh fettuccine
2 tbsps olive oil
2 leeks (white part only), well washed and thinly sliced
500g scallops, roe-on
salt & cracked black pepper, to taste
vodka

Place the wine, saffron strands and cracked pepper in a saucepan and bring to the boil. Reduce heat and simmer until liquid is reduced by half. Add the cream and simmer gently until sauce thickens.

While the sauce is reducing, place the pasta in a large saucepan of salted boiling water and cook until al dente.

Heat oil in a large frypan and sauté the leeks and scallops for approximately 1minute or until just cooked. Add the cream mixture and pasta to the frypan and toss to combine. Season with salt and cracked pepper to taste. Remove frypan from heat and shake a little vodka over the top. Flambé the vodka carefully. Flames should die down in a few seconds. Serve immediately.

CHEF'S TIP: You can add chopped dill to the pasta just before serving.

Oven roasted baby rack of lamb

served on marinated chargrilled vegetables, presented in a crisp pastry tartlet with a salsa verde & garlic aioli

Serves 4

ingredients

4 x 6-chop racks of lamb trimmed & boned cleaned (ask your butcher to do this)
2 tbsps crushed garlic
2 tbsps Dijon mustard
salt & pepper, to taste

chargrilled vegetables
2 tbsps olive oil
1 red capsicum
1 yellow capsicum
1 eggplant & 1 zucchini, sliced
2 tsps crushed garlic
salt & pepper, to taste
1 tbsp apple balsamic vinegar

pastry tartlet
1 ¾ cups plain flour
120g butter
1 egg yolk
30mls cold water
salt

salsa verde
½ bunch parsley
½ bunch basil
½ bunch watercress
3 garlic cloves
3 anchovy fillets
250mls olive oil

garlic aioli
8 garlic cloves
2 egg yolks
1 tsp Dijon mustard
juice of two lemons
salt & pepper, to taste
250mls grape seed oil

To make the tartlet, place flour and butter in a food processor and pulse until mixture resembles fine breadcrumbs. Add egg yolk and water and mix to a firm dough, adding a little more water, if necessary. Turn out onto a floured surface and knead lightly for 2 minutes. Wrap in plastic and refrigerate for 2 hours. Roll pastry onto a floured surface and cut pastry to fit a 10-12cm tart mould. Refrigerate for 30 minutes. Remove from fridge and prick tarts with a fork. Line each tart with some wax paper or foil and fill with dried beans. Bake in preheated oven of 200°C for 12 minutes. Remove the beans and paper and bake for 2-4 minutes more to brown, place on cooling rack.

To make the verde, place all ingredients in a blender and process for 10 seconds or until smooth.

To prepare the aioli, place garlic on a baking tray, drizzle with olive oil and bake in a 180°C oven for 10 minutes or until soft. Place garlic, egg yolks, mustard, lemon juice, salt and pepper in a food processor and process for 10 seconds. With the motor still running, add the oil in a thin stream. When the mixture starts to thicken you can add the oil faster. Continue to process until the mayonnaise is thick and creamy.

To prepare the vegetables, brush capsicums with oil and place on a tray under a hot grill turning occasionally until the skins start to blacken. Place in a bowl and cover. When cool, remove the seeds and skin and cut into 2cm strips. Brush eggplant and zucchini with oil and cook on a hot chargrill or barbecue until soft. Cut into 2cm strips and combine with garlic, salt, pepper, apple balsamic and mix well to combine. For the lamb, place the garlic, mustard, salt, pepper in a bowl and mix well to combine. Rub the mixture into the lamb. Place the lamb on a greased baking tray and bake in a preheated oven of 180°C for about 12 minutes to medium rare. Remove from oven and rest for 5 minutes. Warm tartlets for 1 minute in hot oven.

To serve, place a tartlet on a plate. Fill the middle of each tartlet with the vegetables. Place rack of lamb on top and drizzle with the salsa verde and garlic aioli. Garnish with fresh rosemary or thyme.

Chocolate & coffee

marquise with mixed berry compote and vanilla anglaise

Serves 8-10

ingredients

chocolate & coffee marquise
150g dark chocolate
150g white chocolate
400g unsalted butter
12 egg yolks
1¾ cup castor sugar
30g instant coffee mixed with water to make a paste
2 cups cocoa
600mls cream
½ cup icing sugar

vanilla anglaise
6 egg yolks
⅓ cup sugar
400mls milk
1 vanilla bean
200mls cream

mixed berry compote
500g variety of mixed berries (blueberries, raspberries, blackberries, strawberries – fresh or frozen)
⅔ cup sugar
150mls water

To make the marquise, place dark and white chocolate separately into saucepans and stir over a low heat until smooth. Set aside.

Dice butter and soften to room temperature. Beat the egg yolks & castor sugar in a bowl until pale and thick. Add the butter to the egg yolks in batches, beating after each addition. Transfer ¼ of egg yolk mixture to a second bowl.

Fold coffee paste and melted white chocolate through the egg yolk mixture in the second bowl. Sift cocoa over egg yolk mixture in the first bowl and fold in the melted dark chocolate.

Whip cream and icing sugar in a bowl until soft peaks are formed and add ¼ of the cream to the white chocolate mixture and ¾ of the cream to the dark chocolate mixture. Pour each mixture into a 2 litre container in layers then swirl with knife. Place in freezer for at least 6-8 hours to set.

To make the vanilla anglaise, place egg yolks and sugar in a bowl and mix well to combine. Place milk, vanilla bean and cream in a saucepan and bring to the boil. Remove from heat. Discard the vanilla bean. Add the egg yolks mixture in a slow, continuous stream while whisking then cook slowly over a double boiler, stirring constantly, until the mixture coates the back of a spoon.

To make the compote, place the berries, sugar and water in a saucepan and bring to boil over a medium heat. Remove ½ the berries and set aside. Simmer the remaining berries until reduced to a glaze. Remove from heat and return the other ½ of the berries to the mixture. Set aside and cool.

To serve, place a tablespoon of the mixed berry compote in the middle of a plate. Slice a piece of marquise and place on top. Drizzle a tablespoon of vanilla anglaise over the top. Enjoy....

3 ▶ spicy

Take a deep breath, it's time to drink in that view

The original wharf still stands; a remnant of Port Douglas's past

Stroll down Macrossan Street and find the perfect sidewalk café. Feast on sun-ripened tropical fruits, enjoyed from a comfy chair, with the morning paper.

Find a café that serves exotic tropical fruit juices to waken the taste buds. Sample a *Soursop Magic* or *Cane Toad* (with black sapote), served in tall glasses bursting with tropical vegetation.

Hire a bike and find your way home along landscaped pathways. Palm-lined bike tracks meander through lush resorts. Perhaps you could catch a ride home on the Bally Hooley, a little painted steam train that makes its way through mangrove and landscaped gardens to St Crispin's Station.

In the evenings, Macrossan Street bursts with life; patrons spill onto footpaths, cafes and restaurants line the street as the senses are bombarded with the plethora of entertainments.

Work your way through town at a leisurely pace. Past open-air restaurants with their buzz of animated conversation, their clink of glasses and strains of music carried out into the balmy evening air. Or dine al fresco in courtyards illuminated by torch flame, its glow falling on sun-warmed skin, the air heavy with the scent of night blossoms.

Of course, if you find this over-abundance of eating opportunities a little too demanding, you can always duck into one of Macrossan Street's little day spas for a bit of re-enforcement. A dose of rejuvenative therapy may be necessary at this stage, to help you cope with the rigours of another day in Paradise.

Above left: ancient mangroves line the inlet.
Above right: something about palm fronds.
Opposite: The Old Wharf.

Lines of white yachts from faraway ports

Clockwise from left: the Longest Lunch, Carnivale; dining on the Inlet; Blessing of the fleet, Carnivale. Opposite: Marina Mirage. Previous page: backdrop of pale grey and salmon-streaked sunset.

Make sure you take in the Sunday Markets, nestled in under the shade of a cool mango grove, planted by sailors last century, so they could lie beneath and feed on the fruit until the boats came in. Sample fresh produce from local growers and taste the difference being closer to the food source. See how much richer the flavour of sun ripened tropical fruits. Look for black sapote, passionfruit and wing beans. Gaze beyond the rows of hot lime and chilli sarongs as tall white sails pass through the inlet and out into the Big Blue.

Follow the local tradition and unwind with Margueritas and live music – on Sunday afternoons after the markets.

Stroll along the boardwalks and past the restaurants – white sails against a backdrop of dark and distant mountain peaks.

Clockwise from right: Cactus Bar; Central Hotel;
Courthouse Hotel; Betta Than a Chook Raffle on
sunday afternoons in the courtyard at Salsa Bar &
Grill; Ironbar. Opposite: Michaelangelos.

44

Follow the local tradition
and unwind with a beer and
a band on sunday afternoons

Taking in the Inlet, with sails etched against the soft tones of the horizon

This is where you find that special dive boat or deep-sea fishing experience you've been after.

Lines of white yachts from faraway ports, rigging creaking, salt air and sea lapping. You can take a sunset cruise for some serious crocodile spotting or join in the Wednesday night Sails, armed with BYO champagne and newfound local friends. Sit back and enjoy a pre-dinner cruise for a minimal fee.

Tonight, why not find a restaurant on the Inlet? Make sure you arrive in time to catch the sunset. Take a deep breath and look at that view. There, laid out before you... to take that breath away... against a fairy-lit backdrop of pale grey and salmon-streaked sunset... the perfect seafood sensations await. So, armed with Sauvignon Blanc in one hand, and a fresh prawn or two in the other, it's time to drink in that view.

And as views in Port Douglas go, this would be one of the best – 180 degrees of twilight on the water, taking in the inlet with the sails of a Chinese junk etched against the soft-steely tones of the horizon. You're free to sit back and let the whole therapeutic experience of holidaying in one of the world's premiere gourmet destinations wash over you.

Clockwise from top left: Outrigger team at the entrance to the Inlet; dive boat heads out to the reef; Wine and Food Festival, Carnivale; sunday afternoon dining at Salsa Bar & Grill. Oppostie boats moored on the inlet

47

Gaze beyond the rows of hot lime & chilli sarongs, sun ripened tropical fruits

Take in the Sunday Markets, experience cane toad racing at the Ironbar or catch a ride on the Bally Hooley

Chinese style

roasted duck on a warm salad of flame ginger flower, lychee & water-chestnuts with a mandarin glaze

Serves 4

ingredients

duck
2 whole ducks
4 star anise
2 tbsps szechwan pepper
¼ cup red roast pork seasoning
250g Chinese maltose
¾ cup banana chilli sauce
1 tbsp ginger, finely chopped
2 tbsps sesame oil
100mls Chinese rice wine

mandarin glaze
100mls mandarin
100g castor sugar
40mls rice wine vinegar
30mls fish sauce
1 tbsp ginger, chopped
½ chilli (or to your liking)

stir fry
1 tbsp sesame oil
4 water chestnuts
2 tbsps spanish onion, sliced
2 tbsps lychees, chopped
1 tbsp flame ginger flower, chopped
10 coriander leaves
10 mint leaves
6 bok choy leaves, roughly chopped
salt & pepper, to taste

Blanch whole ducks for 1 minute in a pot of boiling water. Refresh in ice water. Place the star anise and pepper in a mortar and pestle and grind into a fine powder. Rub mixture onto the skin of the blanched ducks. Place the red roast pork seasoning, maltose, banana chilli sauce, ginger, sesame oil and rice wine into a bowl and mix well to combine. Rub half of the seasoning mixture onto the skin of the duck, leaving the other half for basting. Refrigerate for 24 hours. Place ducks on a lightly greased baking tray and bake in a preheated oven of 125°C for approximately 3½ hours or until ducks just start to colour, basting every ½ hour with remaining seasoning mixture. Set aside and cool. Using a large heavy knife or cleaver, chop the duck into portions of legs and breasts.

To make the mandarin glaze, place mandarin, sugar, rice wine vinegar, fish sauce, ginger and chilli into a saucepan and bring to the boil over a high heat. Reduce heat and simmer for 5 minutes then strain and set aside.

Place duck portions onto a baking tray with 600 mls of water and place in a preheated oven of 250°C and bake for 10-15 minutes or until water is just about evaporated.

While ducks are in the oven, heat sesame oil in wok or frypan and when just smoking add chestnuts, onion, lychees, ginger flower, coriander, mint and bok choy and stir-fry for 1-2 minutes. Season with salt & pepper.

To serve, place a portion of the stir-fried vegetables on a plate and top with a leg and breast portion of the duck. Reheat the mandarin sauce and pour over the duck. Garnish with some coriander or finely sliced chilli.

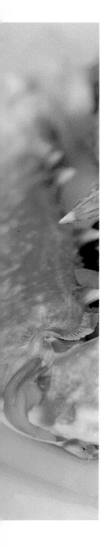

Fried blue swimmer

crab, dressed whole, served on a crispy sprout & bean salad with roast capsicum jam

Serves 4

4 fresh blue swimmer crabs
3 egg whites
½ cup cornflour
1 tsp Hondashi
1 tbsp sesame seeds
oil for deep-frying

stuffing

200g rice vermicelli noodles
reserved crab meat, finely chopped
1 clove garlic, finely chopped
1 tbsp ginger, very finely chopped
1 tbsp coriander, chopped
1 tbsp mint, chopped
1 spring onion (white part only) finely sliced
½ cup coconut cream (do not shake can) cream only
2 tsps lime juice & 1 tsp fish sauce
½ tsp brown sugar

sprout salad

200g bean sprouts
100g green beans, julienned
½ red capsicum, julienned
1 tbsp coriander, chopped
1 tsp sesame oil & 1 tsp fish sauce
¼ cup sweet chilli sauce
1 tbsp lime juice
1 tsp black sesame seeds

roast capsicum jam

1 tbsp sesame oil
2 red capsicums, finely chopped
½ red onion, finely chopped
1 clove garlic, finely chopped
¼ cup sweet chilli sauce
1 tsp fish sauce & 1 tsp soy sauce
1 tbsp coriander leaves, chopped

To make the capsicum jam, heat oil in frypan and add capsicum, onion, garlic and cook until onion is soft. Add the chilli sauce, fish sauce and soy sauce and simmer until mixture thickens slightly. Set aside and, when cooled, add coriander.

Place crabs in a large pot of salted boiling water and simmer, uncovered, for 10 minutes. Remove the crab from the water and set aside and cool. Remove limbs and claws from crabs and extract the meat from the legs but reserve the claws. Open the body without destroying the upper shell which is needed for serving and remove the meat. Rinse out and dry the crab shells.

To make stuffing, soak noodles in boiling water for 1 minute, drain and place in bowl. Add the crab meat, garlic, ginger, coriander, mint, spring onion, coconut cream, lime juice, fish sauce and brown sugar and mix well to combine. Place stuffing into crab shells. Combine the cornflour and Hondashi on a large plate. Dip the crab segments in the seasoning mix then into the egg white mixture then toss to coat in sesame seeds.

Deep-fry the crabs in a wok for 2-3 minutes or until golden brown. Place on absorbent paper and set aside and rest.

To make the salad, combine the beans, capsicum, bean sprouts, coriander, sesame oil, sweet chilli sauce, fish sauce, lime juice and sesame seeds and arrange on a serving plate. Place the stuffed crab shell with claws on top of the salad and drizzle the capsicum jam over the top.

Cajun blackened snapper

fillet on corn and sun dried tomato risotto drizzled with a chervil vin blanc sauce

Serves 4

ingredients
750g snapper fillets
2 tbsps cajun seasoning
1 tbsp oil

corn & sun dried tomato risotto
2 corn cobs, kernels removed
4-5 cups of good-quality fish stock
1 tbsp olive oil
1 tbsp butter
2 cups arborio rice
¼ cup sun dried tomatoes
1 tsp tumeric powder

chervil vin blanc sauce
1 tbsp butter
1 spring onion, finely chopped
½ cup white wine
½ cup good-quality fish stock
⅔ cup cream
drop worchester sauce
1 tbsp chervil

Cut down the corns with a sharp knife to remove the kernels. Dry-fry the kernels over a medium heat shaking the pan regularly until kernels turn golden brown (do not burn). Place stock into a large saucepan and bring to the boil. Reduce heat and keep to a slow simmer. Heat oil and butter in a large heavy based saucepan. Add rice and stir for 1-2 minutes or until transparent. Add 1 cup of stock to the pan and stir constantly over a medium heat until the liquid is absorbed. Continue adding stock, 1 cup at a time, stirring constantly for 20 minutes. Add kernels, sun dried tomatoes and tumeric powder and mix well to combine. Cook for a further 5 minutes or until rice is cooked.

To make the sauce, heat butter in a saucepan. Add spring onion and sauté for 1 minute. Add wine, fish stock and cream and simmer until sauce is creamy but not a thick consistency. Season with salt, pepper and Worchester sauce. Remove from heat and add chervil and mix well to combine. Keep warm.

Coat the snapper fillets with the cajun seasoning. Pour oil into a very hot cast iron frypan (you can also chargrill or barbecue). Place fillets into frypan and cook for 2 minutes on one side then turn over, reduce heat, and cook for approximately 2 minutes on the other side or until the fillets are cooked.

To serve, place a serving of risotto on a plate, top with the snapper and drizzle with the sauce.

CHEF'S TIP: You can substitute the chervil with chinese parsley or fresh coriander in the sauce.

Grilled lamb

loin salad

Serves 4

ingredients
500g boneless lamb loin
1 clove crushed garlic
1 tbsp rosemary, finely chopped
1 tsp cumin
2 tbsps tandoori paste
2 tbsps olive or vegetable oil
200g assorted lettuce leaves
½ medium daikon radish, thinly sliced
2 tsps pickled ginger, roughly chopped
1 punnet cherry tomatoes, quartered or teardrop
1 lebanese cucumber, peeled, seeded & sliced
⅓ cup plain yoghurt

Trim lamb of any fat or sinew (preferably have the butcher do this for you).

Combine garlic, rosemary, cumin, tandoori paste and oil in a large bowl and mix well. Pour mixture over lamb and refrigerate and marinate for at least 2 hours.

Place the lamb on a hot chargrill or barbecue and sear for 1 to 2 minutes on each side or until cooked to medium rare. Set aside to rest for 2 minutes before slicing.

Toss the lamb, radish, ginger, tomatoes, cucumber, lettuce and yoghurt and place on serving plates. Serve immediately.

Chilli mudcrab

Serves 4

ingredients

2 live mudcrab
1 tbsp olive oil
1 tbsp sesame oil
2 stalks lemon grass (white part only), finely chopped
1-2 tsps hot chillis, finely chopped
1 tbsp galangal, finely chopped
1 tsp fresh garlic, finely chopped
1 tbsp ginger, finely chopped
1 tbsp blackbean paste
⅓ cup sweet sherry
⅓ cup ginger wine
500mls good quality fish stock
2 tomatoes, skins removed & chopped
¼ cup coriander leaves, chopped

Place mudcrabs in freezer or iced water for 30 minutes until they are in a state of deep hibernation.

You should now prepare all the other ingredients while the mudcrabs chill out. When you are organised with everything (ready in small bowls, saucers, etc) take a deep breath and begin.

To prepare the crabs, remove the tail flap and lift off the head shell. Scrape away the gills (also called dead man's fingers), along with the eyes and rinse away the crab's innards under cold water. With a heavy knife cut the body in half lengthways and crack the claws.

Now let's get busy - we don't want to burn anything!! Heat the oil in a wok and when oil starts to smoke, carefully add the crab segments and toss for 1-2 minutes to seal. Add the lemon grass, chilli, galangal, garlic, ginger and blackbean paste and keep tossing. Now add the sherry and ginger wine and reduce by half. Add the fish stock and bring to the boil. Reduce the heat and simmer for 10 minutes. Remove crabs and set aside. Add tomatoes and coriander and simmer until sauce thickens.

To serve, divide crab segments into bowls then pour sauce over the crab. Serve with jasmine rice.

You will need fingerbowls, napkins and some chunky fresh bread to mop up all that lovely sauce!

Marinated duck

breast with moroccan couscous, braised leeks & paprika oil

Serves 4

ingredients

4 duck breasts
½ cup sea salt

marinade

1 tbsp chinese five spice
2 tbsps ginger, grated
2 tbsps garlic, finely chopped
1½ tsps rice wine
1 tbsp sugar
½ cup olive oil

braised leeks

4 leeks (white part only), washed & sliced
2 cups chicken stock
¼ cup white wine
2 tbsps lime juice
cracked black pepper

couscous

1½ cups couscous
2 cups chicken stock
1 tbsp butter
2 bocconcini cheese, chopped
3 shallots, finely chopped
1 large red chilli, seeded & finely chopped
½ cup dates, finely chopped
¼ cup semi-dried tomatoes, finely chopped
¼ cup roasted pecans, finely chopped
salt & pepper, to taste

paprika oil

2 tsps paprika
¼ cup olive oil

To prepare the duck, sprinkle salt onto the skin of the duck and refrigerate overnight, uncovered, to draw out moisture.

To make the marinade, place the chinese five spice, ginger, garlic, rice wine, sugar and olive oil in a bowl and mix well to combine. Remove the salt from the duck. Pour the marinade over the duck breasts and refrigerate and marinate for 1 hour. Place the duck on a greased baking tray and bake in a 160°C oven for 20 minutes. Increase oven to 180°C and cook duck for a further 10 minutes until the skin is crispy.

To prepare the leeks, place leeks in a baking tray with the stock, wine, lime juice and pepper and cook for approximately 35 minutes or until soft.

To make the couscous, place the couscous in a large bowl and pour in the boiling stock. Cover tightly with plastic wrap and allow to stand for approximately 5 minutes or until the liquid is absorbed. Mix the couscous well with a fork to separate the granules then add butter, bocconcini cheese, shallots, chilli, dates, semi dried tomatoes, pecans, salt and pepper and mix well to combine.

Place the paprika and oil in a small bowl and mix well to combine.

Place duck on the top of the couscous on a plate and serve with the braised leeks. Drizzle the paprika oil around the plate.

Chargrilled sirloin

with roasted pumpkin galette, serrano chilli hollandaise sauce and chorizo spring roll

Serves 4

ingredients

4 x 300g sirloin steak

roasted pumpkin galette
1 pumpkin, seeded & peeled
500g mashed potato
2 sticks rosemary
¾ cup fine breadcrumbs
salt & pepper, to taste
flour to coat
1 tbsp oil

serrano chilli hollandaise sauce
4 egg yolks
¼ cup champagne vinegar
⅓ cup sweet chilli sauce
500g clarified butter, melted
2 large chillis, seeded & chopped finely
salt & pepper, to taste

chorizo spring roll
3 tbsps oil
150g chorizo sausage, finely chopped
3 tomatoes, finely chopped
1 tbsp fish sauce
1 tbsp sweet soy sauce (kejap manis)
¼ cup coriander, chopped
4 spring roll sheets

To make the galette, place pumpkin on a greased baking tray and roast until very soft. Mash pumpkin into the mashed potato. Add breadcrumbs, rosemary, salt and pepper and mix well to combine. Shape mixture into patties and toss in flour. Heat oil in a non-stick fry-pan and cook galettes on each side over a medium heat until golden brown.

To prepare the spring rolls, heat 1 tablespoon oil in frypan. Add chorizo and cook over a medium heat until golden and crispy. Place on absorbent paper and allow to cool. Place chorizo, tomato, fish sauce, sweet soy sauce and chopped coriander in a bowl and mix well to combine. Lay spring roll wrappers on bench and place a small amount of sausage mix into the centre and roll into spring rolls of 10 cm x 2 cm. Heat remaining oil in frypan and shallow fry until golden brown. Slice spring rolls with a sharp knife on an angle to get two spears.

To make the sauce, place egg yolks, vinegar and chill sauce in a saucepan and whisk constantly over a medium heat until the mixture forms a figure 8 and holds shape for a couple of seconds. Slowly pour in the melted butter whisking vigorously until combined. Remove from heat. Add chillis and season with salt and pepper.

Place steaks on a chargrill or barbecue and cook over a high heat for 1 minute on each side or until they are sealed and seared.

Serve the steaks with a galette and the spring roll spears with a little of the hollandaise sauce drizzled over the steak.

Asian crusted atlantic

salmon with vegetable fritters and garlic aioli

Serves 4

4 x 180g atlantic salmon fillets, skin removed
1 tbsp oil

crust

1 tbsp candlenuts, finely chopped
1 tbsp ginger, finely chopped
1 tbsp fresh tumeric, finely chopped
1 egg beaten

vegetable fritters

1 cup flour
2 eggs, lightly beaten
¾ cup milk
½ tsp fish sauce
1 tbsp oil
¼ cup carrots
¼ cup red onion
¼ cup zucchini
¼ cup celery
all vegetables finely chopped
¼ cup corn kernels
salt & pepper, to taste
¼ cup chopped coriander
¼ cup wombok, sliced
oil, for shallow-frying

garlic aioli

4 garlic cloves
1 tbsp olive oil
2 egg yolks
1 tsp Dijon mustard
1 tbsp lemon juice
salt & pepper, to taste
1 cup grape seed oil

To prepare the aioli, place garlic on a baking tray, drizzle with olive oil and bake in a 180°C oven for 10 minutes or until soft. Place garlic, lemon juice, egg yolks, mustard, salt and pepper in a food processor and process for 10 seconds. With the motor still running, add the oil in a thin stream. When the mixture starts to thicken you can add the oil faster. Continue to process until the mayonnaise is thick and creamy.

To make the fritters, sift flour into a bowl, make well in centre and gradually add eggs, milk and fish sauce. Whisk until smooth. Heat oil in frypan. Add carrots, onion, zucchini, celery, corn, salt and pepper and cook over a medium heat for 2 minutes. Add vegetables, coriander and wombok to batter mixture and mix well to combine.

Heat oil in a non-stick frypan. Drop a tablespoon of the batter and cook on both sides until lightly browned. Set aside and keep warm.

To make the crust, place candlenuts, ginger and tumeric in a bowl and mix well to combine. Brush salmon fillets with egg then coat with crust mixture. Heat oil in frypan and sear for 30 seconds on each side. Place on greased baking tray and cook in preheated oven of 180°C for approximately 5 minutes or until medium rare making sure the crust does not burn.

To serve, place the fritters on a serving plate and top with the salmon. Drizzle the garlic aioli over the top.

Asian prawns

on sugarcane sticks

Serves 4

400g raw prawn meat, finely chopped
¾ cup coriander leaves, chopped
3 stems lemon grass (white part only), very finely sliced
1 tsp fish sauce
2 cloves crushed garlic
1 tsp sesame oil
2 egg whites
salt and pepper, to taste
sesame seeds, for coating
peanut oil, for deep-frying
sugar cane chopsticks (see recipe)

dipping sauce

1 tbsp lime juice
2 tsps fish sauce
1 tbsp soy sauce
1 cup spring onions, finely chopped
2 red chillies, deseeded & chopped finely
1 tbsp Mirin rice wine

Combine prawn meat, coriander, lemon grass, fish sauce, garlic, sesame oil, egg whites, salt and pepper in a bowl and mix well. Cut sugar cane into pieces to resemble chopsticks. Mould a portion of the prawn mixture around the end of the sticks. (You can also shape prawn mixture into balls if sugar cane not available) Toss to coat in sesame seeds. Heat oil in a deep saucepan and add prawns in batches and deep-fry over medium-high heat for 1 minute or until golden brown.

To make the sauce, place lime juice, fish sauce, soy sauce, onions, chillis and rice wine and mix well to combine.

Serve prawn sticks with a small bowl of the dipping sauce.

4 ▶ deep

Light hits the surface, you're free to
fly deeper and discover more of nature's secrets

You're flying, suspended above a brilliant wash of colours, a dazzling blur of fluorescents

If you visit in Spring, the visibility underwater is up to 40 metres on the outer reefs. For the ultimate dive experience, there are 3000 reefs to choose from in the total barrier reef system and by no means are they all the same. Each can be a different adventure.

Dive from your boat, and you enter another world. 350 different species of coral, 400 different species of sponges, over 4000 different species of mollusc – and 1500 species of fish.

You're flying, suspended above a brilliant wash of colours. The vibrancy of those colours – in both the coral and the fish – is highlighted by beams of sunlight cutting crisply through the cool blue.

Plunge deeper through sun-warmed surface into cool darkened depths. A new land is spread before you, teeming with life. One flick of your flipper and you're gliding effortlessly past this melange of coloured life forms.

You're free to fly deeper and discover more of nature's secrets. Gazing up towards the surface, shards of sunlight leak their milky glow, as the slow black of turtle silhouette passes overhead.

Clockwise from top left: a pair of Anemonefish; humpback whale breach; Longnose Butterflyfish (Forcipiger longirostris). Opposite: snorkelling at Low Isles, photograph by Stephen Nutt.

71

Leaving you overwhelmed by the artistry of nature's palette

Clockwise from top: beams of sunlight cut through plate coral formations (Acropora sp.); an aerial view of the outer reef, photograph by Stephen Nutt; Maori Wrasse (Cheilinus undulates). Opposite: a vivid display of soft coral (Dendronephthya sp.)

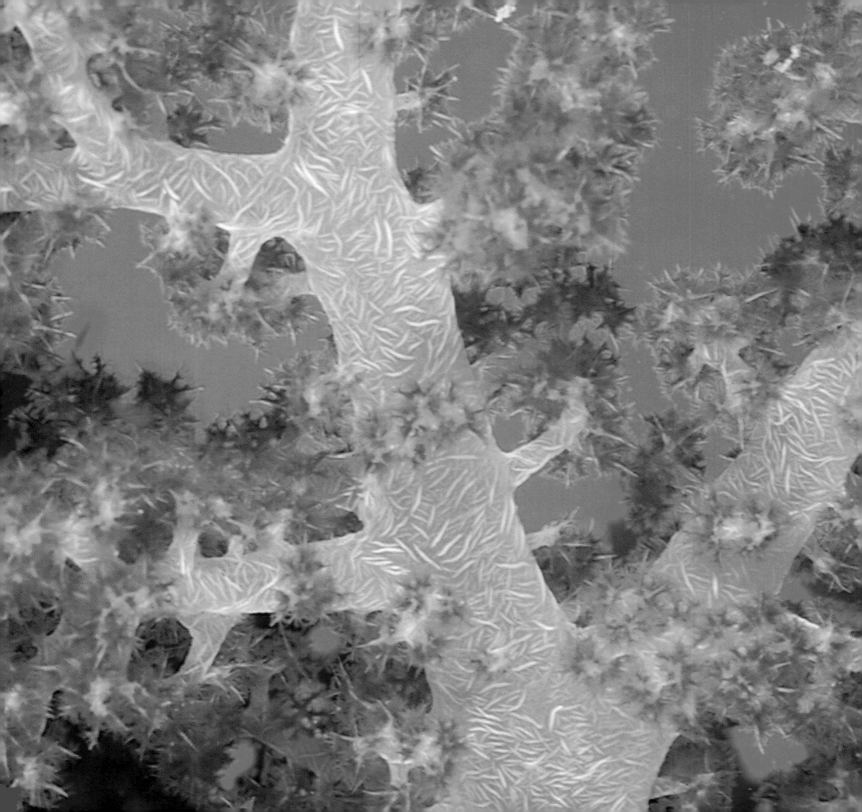

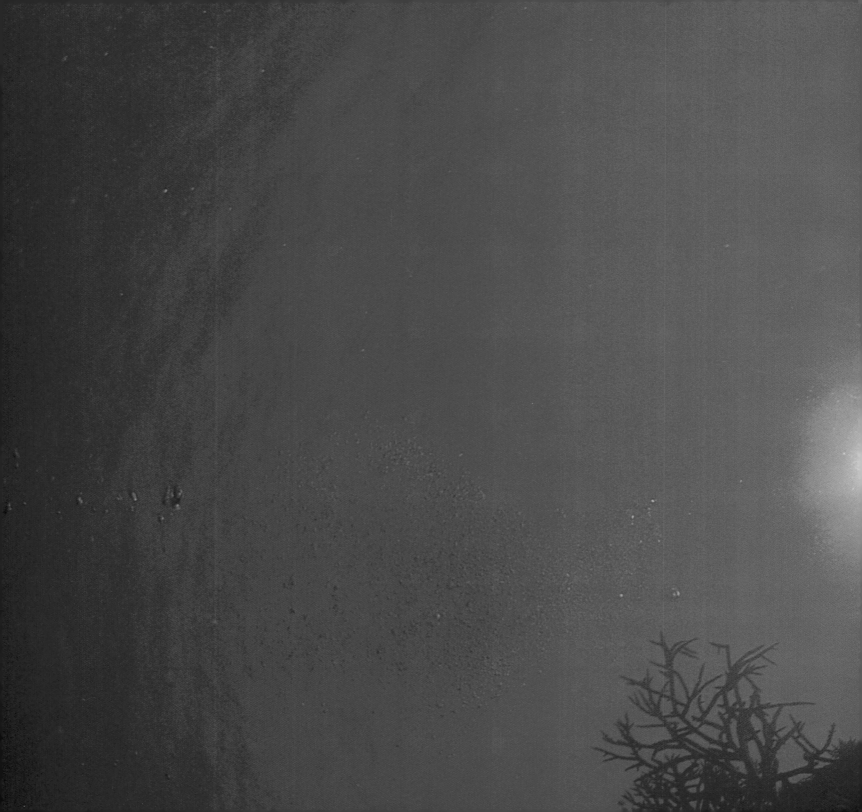

Plunge deeper through sun-warmed surface into cool darkened depths

Light hits the surface like mercury rolling above as you turn to explore this other world. The bright yellow trumpet fish passes by like a character from Walt Disney's Fantasia. Soft terracotta coral trout with electric-blue freckles clash with neon-lit lemon and silver-striped sea perch.

Watch the tiny Cleaner Wrasse work their magic, busily clearing fungi and parasites from the larger fish at special grooming stations. Schools of Golden Damsel and Fairy Basslets flash past in a dazzling blur of fluorescence, through coral polyps and featherstars, leaving you overwhelmed by the artistry of nature's palette.

Clockwise from above right: Imperial Angelfish (Pomacanthus imperator); a diver floats amongst a deep crevasse of coral formation; Lace coral (Stylaster sp.) Opposite: underwater world. Previous page: Plunge deeper through sun-warmed surface into cool darkened depths.

A flick of your flipper and you're gliding effort-lessly past this melange of coloured life forms

Clockwise from top: soft coral (Dendronephthya); school of Glass fish; Anemone fish being protected by the poisonous ten-tacles of the Anemone; a Dugong. Opposite: Anthias or Fairy Basslets break out with an explosion of colour over a coral nursery bommie.

Highlighted by beams of sunlight cutting crisply through the cool blue

Clockwise from top:
Whitetip Reef shark
(Triaenodon obesus);
Staghorn coral
formation (Acropora
sp.); the legendary
Cod Hole near Lizard
Island. Opposite:
Ctenophor Comb
Jellyfish.

Salt and pepper

squid with

cucumber

& mint salad

Serves 4

ingredients

12 small squid, cleaned and cut into triangles
1/2 pawpaw, diced
cornflour for coating
oil, for deep-frying
3 tsps sea salt
1 tsp szechwan peppercorns
1 tsp white pepper
250g assorted lettuce leaves
1 cucumber, peeled, seeds removed and sliced thinly
1 red onion, sliced thinly
1 cup shredded mint
100g bean sprouts

dressing

2 tbsps maize oil
2 cloves crushed garlic
1 large red chilli, seeded & finely chopped
1 stalk lemon grass, white part only, finely chopped
2 tbsps lime juice or 2 finely shredded kaffir lime leaves
2 tbsps lemon juice
1 tbsp palm sugar or soft brown sugar
1 tbsp fish sauce

Score one side of the squid with the tip of a sharp knife. Place the squid and pawpaw in a bowl and mix well. Refrigerate and marinate for at least 2 hours. Remove the squid from the marinade and wash and pat dry. Toss the squid in cornflour. Heat the oil in a deep saucepan over a medium-high heat. Add the squid in small batches and cook for approximately 20-30 seconds, or until golden. Drain on absorbent paper.

Place the salt and peppers in a dry frying pan and toast over a medium heat for 5 minutes. Sift the salt and pepper mixture over the top of the squid pieces and mix well to combine.

Toss the lettuce, cucumber, onion, mint and bean sprouts and place on serving plates. Top with the squid pieces.

To make dressing, place all the ingredients in a bowl and mix well to combine. Pour dressing over salad and serve.

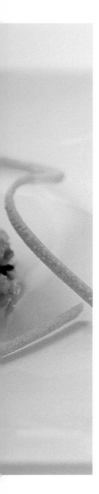

Swordfish with sorrel

gnocchi and sweet chilli bay bug on a roma tomato & capsicum salsa

Serves 4

ingredients

4 x 180g fresh swordfish fillets (not frozen)
flour, for coating
1 tbsp butter
⅓ cup grated parmesan cheese

sorrel gnocchi

4 large potatoes
1 egg yolk
½ bunch sorrel, finely chopped
125g plain flour
1 tbsp butter
salt & pepper, to taste

sweet chilli bay bug

¼ cup sweet chilli sauce
2 cloves crushed garlic
1 tbsp castor sugar
salt & finely ground black pepper, to taste
4 bay bug tail meat

roma tomato & capsicum salsa

2 red capsicums
2 roma tomatoes, seeds removed & finely chopped
½ bunch fresh coriander, chopped
1 brown onion, finely chopped
½ cup olive oil
salt & pepper, to taste

To prepare the bay bugs, combine sweet chilli sauce, garlic, sugar, salt and pepper in a bowl. Add the bug tail meat and mix to combine. Refrigerate and marinate for 15 minutes.

To prepare the Salsa, place whole capsicums on a tray under a hot grill. Cook, turning occasionally, until the skin starts to blacken. Place the capsicums in a bowl covered with plastic wrap. When cool, remove the skins. Cut the capsicums in half, remove the seeds and finely chop. Combine the capsicum, tomato, coriander, onion, and oil olive in a bowl and season with salt and pepper.

To make Gnocchi, wrap potatoes in foil then place on baking tray and bake at 180°C for 45 minutes or until soft. Remove foil and potato skins and mash. Add egg yolk and sorrel and mix well to combine. Stir through flour until a soft dough forms. Form mixture into balls. Press fork on one side to indent. Allow to stand for 15 minutes. Place the gnocchi into a large saucepan of salted boiling water and cook until the gnocchi floats. Drain and toss with butter and season with salt and pepper.

Heat oil in frypan. Add bug tail meat and cook over a medium heat for approximately 1-2 minutes on each side. Lightly coat the Swordfish in flour. Heat butter in frypan. Add fish and cook over medium heat for approximately 2 minutes on each side or until tender.

To serve, spoon the salsa onto the plate, top with gnocchi and a swordfish fillet finishing with the bug tail meat. Sprinkle the parmesan cheese over the top if desired.

CHEF'S TIP: You can substitute the swordfish with mahi mahi, spanish mackerel or tuna.

Baby octopus

salad with mediterranean vegetables and a basil & lime vinaigrette

Serves 4

ingredients
*500g baby octopus, cleaned
1 clove garlic, finely chopped
2 tbsps sesame oil
3 tbsps oyster sauce
salt & pepper, to taste
150g rocket leaves
¼ cup pine nuts, oven roasted
until golden brown
¼ cup parmesan cheese
shavings*

mediterranean vegetables
*1 red capsicum, sliced
1 zucchini, sliced
1 small eggplant, sliced
1 red onion, sliced
olive oil
salt and pepper, to taste*

basil & lime vinaigrette
*juice of 2 limes
1 small red onion, finely
chopped
⅓ cup champagne or white
wine vinegar
⅓ cup extra virgin olive oil
½ cup basil, finely shredded
½ cup parsley, finely chopped
1 tbsp castor sugar
salt & pepper, to taste*

parmesan cheese sticks
*1 sheet puff pastry, cut into 1
cm wide strips
¼ cup grated parmesan cheese
2 egg yolks*

Place octopus, garlic, sesame oil, and oyster sauce in a bowl and mix well. Season with salt and pepper. Refrigerate and marinate for at least 3 hours.

Place puff pastry strips on greaseproof paper on a baking tray. Sprinkle cheese over each strip of pastry. Hold one of the ends of the pastry strips and twist until a spiral forms. Brush each strip with egg yolk and bake in a preheated oven of 200°C for 10 minutes. Turn strips over and cook for another 5 minutes.

Brush capsicum, zucchini, eggplant and onion with oil and cook both sides on a preheated hot chargrill or barbecue until soft. Season with salt and pepper.

Place the octopus on a preheated hot chargrill or barbeque for 2 to 3 minutes or until cooked.

To make vinaigrette, combine lime juice, onion, vinegar, oil, basil, parsley, sugar, salt and pepper and mix well to combine.

Combine rocket leaves, roasted pine nuts and parmesan cheese with baby octopus, mediterranean vegetables and a desired amount of the vinaigrette on a serving plate and top with the cheese sticks.

Seared tuna salad

Serves 4

ingredients

400g tuna fillet
salt & pepper, to taste
1 tbsp lemon juice
4 poached eggs

salad

100g potatoes, chopped
100g green beans, cut into
short pieces
100g yellow beans, cut into
short pieces
150g roma tomatoes,
chopped
1 red onion, finely chopped
60g black pitted olives
80mls extra virgin olive oil
20mls red wine vinegar

coulis

1 tbsp olive oil
½ brown onion, finely
chopped
3 red capsicums, finely
chopped
2 cloves crushed garlic
2 sprigs thyme, finely
chopped
1 tsp sugar
1 cup chicken stock

To prepare the coulis, heat oil in frypan. Add onion and capsicums and cook over a medium heat until soft. Add garlic, thyme and sugar and cook for 2 minutes. Add chicken stock and simmer gently for about 30 minutes. Set aside and allow to cool. Place capsicum mixture in blender and blend until smooth. Press through a sieve.

To make the salad, place potatoes in a pot of boiling water and cook for 5 minutes or until cooked. Drain and cool. Blanch beans in boiling water, drain and cool. Place the potatoes, beans, onion, olives, tomatoes, olive oil and vinegar in a bowl and toss to combine.

Cut tuna into 4 even pieces. Season with salt, pepper and lemon juice. Heat oil in frypan. Gently add tuna and cook for 6 seconds on all sides. Remove and cool slightly.

Place eggs in simmering water and poach for 3-4 minutes.

Slice and place the tuna on top of the salad on a plate then gently place the poached egg and serve with the capsicum coulis.

HAGEN WITTNER | *sheraton mirage resorts*

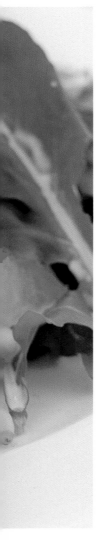

Chargrilled ocean trout

with rocket, orange & almond salad

Serves 4

4 x 180g ocean trout
1 tbsp oil
¼ cup almond flakes
150g rocket leaves
2 oranges, peeled &
segmented
1 tbsp balsamic vinegar
1 tbsp olive oil

breadcrumb mixture

2 cups fine dry breadcrumbs
1 cup grated Italian parmesan
cheese
3 cloves crushed garlic
½ tsp dry chilli (optional)
½ cup Italian parsley,
chopped
2 tbsps fennel leaves,
chopped
2 tbsps chives, sliced
1 tsp salt
¼ tsp ground black pepper

orange aioli

3 egg yolks
1 tsp Dijon mustard
2 tbsps white wine vinegar
2 tbsps fresh orange juice
zest of 1 lemon, grated
zest of 1 orange, grated
1 clove crushed garlic
1 cup canola oil
salt & pepper, to taste

To make the aioli, combine egg yolks, mustard, vinegar, orange juice, the lemon and orange zests and garlic in a bowl and whisk. Add the oil in a slow, continuous stream while whisking until the mayonnaise is thick and creamy. Season with salt and pepper.

Combine breadcrumbs, parmesan cheese, garlic, chilli (optional), parsley, fennel, chives, salt and pepper in a bowl and mix to combine. Lightly coat the fish in the breadcrumbs. The absolutely best way to cook this dish is over very hot coals on a wire rack or barbecue. The hotter the fire, the better. Cook the fish on each side for about 30 seconds or until cooked.

Heat oil in a frypan. Toast almonds over a medium heat for 30 seconds or until golden brown. Toss with the rocket leaves, orange slices, balsamic vinegar and oil.

Serve the fish with the tossed salad then drizzle a little orange aioli over the top.

I first came upon this recipe when a very large Italian man, who went by the name Anaclato, coated some pieces of fish in a mixture of breadcrumbs and Parmesan cheese and cooked them over a fire. It was an event that changed my perception of cooking profoundly. It was a simple dish to prepare and looked rather ordinary. But the secret of why it tasted so good is a secret and I do not have a recipe for it. This recipe is a variation of that particular dish. You can cook any kind of fish in this way; just choose the freshest and firmest looking fish.

Open raviolo

with smoked red emperor and exotic mushrooms

Serves 4

ingredients

1 quantity pasta dough (see recipe)
500g mixed exotic mushrooms (incl. wood ear, oyster, shiitaki & enoki)
¼ bunch fresh chives, chopped
1 tbsp lemon zest
250g smoked Red Emperor wing removed from the bone & shredded
⅔ cup olive oil
1 cup white wine
150g butter
1 cup cream
salt & pepper to taste
small jar salmon caviar
¼ bunch fresh chives cleaned & left whole for garnish

pasta dough

250g plain flour
4 eggs
2 tsps salt
1 tbsp olive oil
¼ cup water

To make the pasta dough, place flour, eggs, salt, oil and water in a bowl and mix well to combine. Turn onto floured surface and knead for approximately 10 minutes into a smooth ball. Wrap in cling wrap and rest for 20 minutes. Using a bench top pasta maker, roll pasta to final thickness of no.6. Cut pasta into circles of 14cm diameter, allowing 2 discs per serve. Place a large saucepan of water on high heat ready for the pasta.

Prepare the filling by sautéing the mushrooms, chives, lemon zest and red emperor in the olive oil, then deglaze the pan with the white wine. Add butter, cream, salt and pepper. Reduce to moderate heat until a creamy texture. While this is reducing, cook the pasta discs for 2 minutes. Strain in colander.

Place bottom disc on the pasta plate, portion mushroom mixture over each disc, reserving some of the liquid for the top. Cover with top disc of pasta and drizzle remaining cream sauce over the top. Garnish with a spoon of salmon caviar and whole chives.

CHEF'S TIP: if there are only 2 of you, freeze uncooked pasta discs with a layer of cling wrap between and reduce the mushroom quantity. You can also substitute the red emperor wings with a variety of smoked fish such as salmon or mackerel.

Orange & almond torte

Serves 6-8

ingredients

2 oranges
300g blanched almonds
1 tsp baking powder
6 eggs
200g castor sugar

chocolate ganache
200g plaistowe dark
cooking chocolate
½ cup cream

orange cointreau sauce
(optional)
2 cups water
1 cup castor sugar
zest of 2 oranges
Cointreau, to taste

Place oranges in a saucepan and cover with cold water. Bring to the boil, reduce heat, cover, and simmer for 2 hours.

Discard water and set aside the oranges to cool. Remove the seeds (if any). Process the almonds and baking powder in a food processor until consistency resembles crushed nuts. Set aside. Process the oranges (skin and all) in food processor until smooth. Beat eggs and sugar in a bowl until light and fluffy. Fold both the orange and almond mixture into the egg and sugar mixture. Pour the mixture into a greased 26 cm (10 inch) spring form tin lined with non-stick baking paper. Preheat oven to 160°C and bake for 1 hour or until cooked when tested with a skewer. Allow cake to settle for 10 minutes before removing from tin. Turn onto a wire rack to cool.

To make ganache, place chocolate in a food processor and process until chocolate resembles course breadcrumbs. Heat cream in a saucepan over a low heat and do not boil. Remove cream from heat and slowly add to chocolate mixture processing until smooth. Immediately spread the ganache over the cooled torte.

To make the sauce, place water, sugar and zest into a saucepan and bring to the boil. Reduce heat and cook over a low heat until sauce becomes syrupy. Add cointreau to taste.

Serve with a dollop of cream and a little of the syrup drizzled over the top.

5 ▶ fresh

Shards of sunlight leak their milky glow

Enjoy the drop in temperature, lounging in the shade with no sound other than the calls of rainforest birds and the deep gurgle of rapids

Clockwise from top right: Mossman Gorge; a buttressed-root fig; crystal clear water streams over granite boulders leaving mint green pools; a Golden Orb spider. Opposite: graphic detail of a Cycad.

Strangler figs shade the palms and ferns beneath in this forest, filled with spirits of their ancestors

"…In the beginning the land was flat…" So say the Kuku Yalanji people, the area's original caretakers. "Kuriyala the Rainbow Python came weaving his way through the landscape, and the rivers and the valleys were formed. Kuriyala possessed healing powers and created special healing pools in the rainforest. Great boulders surrounded some of these pools; these were his eggs and it was forbidden to swim near them." [1].

Some of the resorts in the rainforest utilise these traditional healing pools in creating the most spectacular environment for your stay in the rainforest. Take advantage of the Healing Waters Day Spa – you leave the outside world completely behind. Many of the treatments used have been developed in collaboration with tribal elders.

Cool spring water tumbles down, out of the mountains – streaming over moss-covered boulders, slipping under the forest canopy to leave deep mint-green pools.

1. CJ Fischer; p 55-56 Lloyd Nielsen - Daintree, Jewel of Tropical North Queensland (c) 1997.

Left: Strangling Fig and above: a slice of the forest.
Opposite Mossman Gorge. Previous page: Mossman Gorge.

Enjoy the drop in temperature. Note the change from coastal saltiness. Bring a picnic and spread your blanket, lounging in the shade with no sound other than the calls of rainforest birds and the deep gurgle of rapids. Strangler figs shade the palms and ferns beneath – the forest is festooned with hanging orchids, and bedecked with mosses and lichens.

The custodians of this area, the Kuku Yalanji, will take tourists through their traditional rainforest paths to visit their own special places. For some it will be the most memorable experience of their visit, to have the chance to connect with the people who not only trace a direct lineage of local ancestry through to pre-history but who see this forest as being filled with the spirits of their ancestors.

Find a guide to take you through their sacred land, and share their stories about its origins. One such story tells how the Kuku Yalanji learned what food could be taken from the rainforest and what food was safe to eat. The spirit Kubirri appeared to them in human form and showed them how to treat poisonous seeds to make them edible.

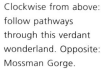

Clockwise from above: follow pathways through this verdant wonderland. Opposite: Mossman Gorge.

Chilled smoked salmon

lasagna with a tomato salsa and saffron, caper & honey dressing

Serves 4

ingredients

250g quality smoked salmon
250g baby english spinach leaves
½ cup marscarpone
½ cup pouring cream
4 basil leaves, shredded
salt & pepper, to taste

pasta dough

300g plain flour
150g semolina
1 tbsp olive oil
pinch salt
2 eggs

saffron, caper & honey dressing

2 tsps Dijon mustard
10 saffron strands
1 tbsp honey
2 tbsps cider vinegar
3 tbsps vegetable oil
3 tbsps olive oil
20 baby capers

tomato salsa

2 tomatoes, finely chopped
½ continental cucumber, seeded & finely chopped
½ spanish onion, finely chopped

To make the pasta, place the flour, semolina, salt, oil and eggs in a food processor and pulse until the dough just comes together. You may need to add 1 tablespoon of water. Knead for 5 minutes with your hands until the dough is smooth and elastic and is dry to touch. Cover dough with plastic wrap then allow to rest for 15 minutes. Roll the dough out on a lightly floured surface as thinly as possible (or use a pasta rolling machine). Place the pasta sheets in a large saucepan of salted boiling water and cook for approximately 5-7 minutes or until al dente. Refresh the pasta sheets by placing in a bowl of iced water then remove, dry and lightly brush with oil on each side. Cut the pasta sheets into required sizes and set aside (you can use a bread or cake tin or individual greased ramekins).

Blanch the spinach leaves then refresh by placing in a bowl of iced water then set aside.

Combine the marscarpone, cream and basil in a bowl and mix well. Add a pinch of salt & pepper to taste.

To assemble the dish, place a pasta sheet on the base, then a slice of smoked salmon, then a layer of the marscarpone cream mixture, then a layer of blanched spinach leaves. Repeat this procedure 3 times finishing with a layer of pasta sheet. Refrigerate for 1 hour before serving.

To prepare the dressing, place mustard, saffron strands, honey, cider vinegar, vegetable oil, olive oil and baby capers in a bowl and mix well to combine.

To make the salsa, place the tomato, cucumber and onion in a small bowl and add a little of the dressing. Mix well to combine.

To serve, place a portion of the lasagna in the centre of a serving plate. Top with the salsa, then pour the dressing over the top and around the plate.

CHEF'S TIP: Pre-made dried lasagna sheets can also be used successfully.

Pan-fried prawns

*and scallops
on fresh italian
style spinach
and melon
viniagrette*

Serves 4

ingredients
*⅓ onion
1 clove garlic
10g sardines cooked in brine,
finely chopped
1 tbsp olive or vegetable oil
1 tsp sesame oil
12 prawns, heads removed,
peeled & deveined
20 scallops
1 ¾ cup cream
400g washed and blanched
baby spinach
salt & pepper, to taste
balsamic vinegar, extra*

melon vinaigrette
*watermelon, honey dew
melon and rockmelon,
finely chopped to make
approximately 1 cup
2 tbsps extra virgin olive oil
1 tbsp balsamic vinegar
salt & pepper, to taste*

Place melons, oil and balsamic vinegar in a bowl and mix well to combine. Season with salt and pepper. Refrigerate and set aside for 30 minutes.

Place onion, garlic and sardines in a blender and process until a smooth paste is formed. Heat oils in frypan. Add prawns and scallops and cook over a medium heat for 1-2 minutes on each side or until cooked. Remove prawns and scallops from pan and keep warm. Add paste to same frypan and cook for 1 minute. Add cream and spinach and simmer for 5 minutes or until mixture is combined. Season with salt and pepper.

Arrange the prawns, scallops and spinach on a serving plate with the vinaigrette. Drizzle a little of balsamic vinegar around the plate.

Coral trout ceviche

and rice noodle salad

Serves 4

ingredients

200g fresh coral trout fillet, sliced thinly as possible
1 tbsp ginger, finely chopped
1 red chilli, seeded & finely chopped
¼ bunch coriander, finely chopped
½ stalk lemon grass (white part only), finely chopped
juice of 3 lemons
⅓ cup coconut milk
1 very green banana, thinly sliced
salt

rice noodle salad

100g rice sticks noodle, cooked & rinsed
100g wood ear mushrooms, finely chopped
½ cup paw-paw, finely chopped
½ red capsicum, finely chopped
1 roma tomato, finely chopped
¼ cup coriander, chopped
¼ cup mint leaves, chopped
¼ cup freshly grated coconut (or desiccated coconut)
¼ cup celery leaves, finely chopped

dressing

⅓ cup sweet chilli sauce
juice of 2 limes & 2 lemons
¼ cup coriander leaves, chopped
1 tbsp palm or brown sugar
½ red chilli, seeded & finely chopped
¼ tsp fish sauce, to taste

To prepare the ceviche, place ginger, chilli, coriander, lemon grass, lemon juice, coconut milk and salt in a bowl and mix well. Pour over the coral trout and refrigerate and marinate overnight or 2 hours if you prefer the "raw" texture of the fish.

To make the dressing, place the sweet chilli sauce, lime juice, lemon juice, coriander leaves, palm sugar, chilli and fish sauce in a blender and blend thoroughly. Keep refrigerated.

To put the salad together, soak noodles in boiling water for 1 minute, drain and place in bowl. Add mushrooms, paw-paw, capsicum, tomato, coriander, mint leaves, grated coconut, celery leaves and a little of the dressing and mix well to combine. Divide the mixture into 4 round moulds to shape and refrigerate for 1 hour.

Deep-fry banana slices in oil over a high heat until golden brown and crisp. Drain on absorbent paper.

Place noodle salad on plate and top with a few slices of coral trout and crispy fried banana. Drizzle a little more of the dressing around the plate.

Fish trio

*with pickled
vegetables and
wasabi cream*

Serves 4

ingredients
*200g swordfish
200g atlantic salmon
200g yellow fin tuna
3 sheets nori
4 sheets spring roll pastry
1 egg white
vegetable oil, for deep-frying
wasabi
soy sauce*

pickled ginger & vegetables
*½ cup white wine vinegar
½ cup rice vinegar
½ cup mirin
¾ cup sugar
1 carrot, julienned
1 continental cucumber,
unpeeled, deseeded &
julienned
5 cm piece ginger, thinly
sliced*

To make the pickled vegetables, place rice vinegar, white wine vinegar, mirin and sugar in a small saucepan and bring to the boil then simmer for 3 minutes or until sugar dissolves. Set aside and allow to cool. Place carrot, cucumber and ginger in a bowl. Add the pickling mixture ensuring that the vegetables are submerged. Seal and refrigerate overnight.

To make the fish trio, cut each fish into 4 strips approximately 10 cm long. Cut each nori sheet into 4 pieces the same width as the fish strips. Brush the nori sheets with egg white. Place each fish strip on a strip of nori and roll the nori up firmly. Press the nori edges together to seal.

Cut the pastry sheets in half. Place 1 pastry sheet on a board and brush with egg white. Place another sheet on top and brush again with the egg white. Place a swordfish, salmon and tuna nori roll on a pastry sheet and roll up firmly. Press the edges together to seal. Repeat the operation.

Deep-fry the "trio" for approximately 45 seconds, or until the pastry is crispy, ensuring that the fish remains uncooked.

To serve, place the "trio" onto a serving dish with the pickled vegetables, wasabi and soy sauce served on the side.

Vegetable frittata

Serves 6-8

ingredients

2 tbsps olive oil
4 zucchini, sliced
2 red onions, finely chopped
4 potatoes, thinly sliced
1 sweet potato, thinly sliced
8 eggs
1 cup grated parmesan cheese
½ cup grated tasty cheddar cheese
1 cup basil, finely chopped
¼ bunch chopped oregano
salt & pepper, to taste
2 vine-ripened tomatoes, sliced thinly
2 tbsps basil, shredded

Heat oil in large frypan. Add zucchini and cook over a moderate heat for approximately 2-3 minutes or until lightly golden. Arrange a layer of zucchini onto a greased baking dish. Add onion and sauté until soft. Sprinkle onion over the zucchini. Cook potatoes for 8-10 minutes or until golden then repeat the process with the sweet potato. Arrange the potato and sweet potato on top of the zucchini and onion.

Place eggs, parmesan cheese, cheddar cheese, basil, oregano, salt and pepper in a bowl and mix well to combine. Pour mixture over layered vegetables. Place in preheated oven of 180°C for 45 minutes. Remove from oven and place a thin layer of tomatoes on top. Sprinkle with basil. Bake in oven of 200°C for a further 10 minutes or until brown on top. Serve warm or cold.

CHEF'S TIP: You may need to place the frittata under the grill for 1-2 minutes to brown on top.

Buttermilk summer

pudding

Serves 6

ingredients
400mls cream
350g castor sugar
1-2 vanilla beans, split
9 gelatine leaves (sheets)
1200mls buttermilk

black cherries in brandied syrup
2 x 425g can black cherries
1 cup castor sugar
Brandy, to taste

Place half the cream, sugar and split vanilla bean in a saucepan and cook over a low heat stirring constantly until sugar dissolves, then remove from heat (ensure not to boil). Remove the vanilla bean then scrape the vanilla seeds into the cream mixture and discard bean skin. Whisk to combine. Soften the gelatine leaves in cold water, squeeze out any excess water and whisk into cream and sugar mix until dissolved. Slowly add the buttermilk whisking constantly until combined. In a separate bowl beat the remaining cream until light and creamy then add to buttermilk mixture and mix well to combine. Pour the mixture into a large mould and refrigerate for at least 8 hours. (You can also use 1 cup capacity dariole moulds).

Separate the cherries from the syrup and set aside. Place the syrup from the cherries and sugar in saucepan and simmer until sauce is reduced. Add brandy to taste. Set aside and cool. Combine the syrup with the cherries.

Unmould pudding and serve with the black cherries in the syrup. You can also use any other berries such as blueberries, blackberries, raspberries or strawberries.

CHEF'S TIP: Whole cherries hold their shape but seedless makes for easy eating.

6 ▶ lush

stark light slices through fan palms

Follow its deep green course, cruise the interior
deeper into the seemingly impenetrable jungle

Clockwise from top
left: Kingfisher; the
steely eye of a
saltwater crocodile;
saltwater crocodile
waits in its under-
water murkiness;
Scrub or Amethistin
python (Morelia
amethistina).
Opposite:
Daintree river.

He taught them about the seasons. When the curtain
fig flowers, it is time to find scrub fowl eggs in their
nesting mounds. When the wattle flowers, it signals
the time to fish for mullet in the river. When the scrub
turkeys migrate to the coast, the blue-fruited ginger
is ripe.

The rainforest gave the people their medicines, it gave
them milky pinesap to stun the fish and make them
easy to catch. It gave them green ginger leaves to
wrap the meat for their earthen ovens.

The Kuku Yalanji feasted on tropical fruits… on bandi-
coots and tree kangaroos… and on cassowaries and
scrub fowl. From the sea, they harvested fish, shell-
fish, turtles – and their favourite, the dugong. In the
end, Kuku Yalanji people are returned to the forest,
their spirits living in the trees… the rocks… in the
forest animals. For the rest of time, they watch over
and protect the tribe.

Watch as the endless rich greens of the rainforest slide by

Driving north from Port Douglas, past cane fields and coconut palms, past Mossman and the burnt molasses smell of the Sugar Mill, the road is lined with aromatic grasses, warm and fragrant in the sun. Soon you'll be catching glimpses of the sea as the road winds its way on to Daintree.

Daintree River was proclaimed by one early explorer to be the most beautiful tropical river he had ever seen, and soon became well known for its stands of white cedar and the untold riches they represented. By the early 20th century, residents were complaining that there should be some kind of control placed on the "reprehensible" timber cutters gouging their way into the virgin wilderness.

These days the Daintree River is more popular with those wanting to explore its crocodile-infested murkiness, to cruise the interior deeper into the seemingly impenetrable jungle – from the secure comfort of their boat. Follow through its deep green course, the surface still save for the lapping of the water. Watch as the endless rich greens of the rainforest slide by, interrupted only by the occasional electric blue or green flash of Ulysses and Birdwing butterflies.

This is where the jungle is thick, and wandering off the beaten track means getting caught up in lawyer cane and Wait-a-While creeper. Stark light slices through fan palms and the air rings with the clear calls of birdsong. Heavy with the smell of damp leaf mould and fresh earth, this forest is home to the Cassowary, a pre-historic looking bird that can stand up to six feet in height. It's worth avoiding.

Clockwise from left: male Eclectus Parrot; fan palms (Licuala Ramsayi) reach for the heavens. Opposite: White lipped tree frog. Previous page: Alexandra Range Lookout.

Clockwise from left: female
Eclectus Parrot; Cassowary;
cruise the Daintree River.
Opposite: Fan Palm Café
and Boardwalk.

Stark light
slices
through fan
palms and
the air rings
with the
clear calls of
birdsong

Clockwise from left: Cooper Creek; Rocky Point; nature imitates art at Cooper Creek. Opposite: Coconut Beach. Previous page: Cape Tribulation, that perfect white sandy beach with no footprints but your own.

Further north where the road carves its way through the rainforest, you'll find Cape Tribulation and that perfect white sandy beach with no footprints but your own.

Here the salty smell of the sea meets the earthiness of the rainforest. Right here, this band of sand draws the line between them.

Follow the decked pathways that lead you through the mangroves – suspending you above their ancient root systems and the murky mud-crab worlds below – and leading you out of their shady shelter into the clear blast of blue water and white light.

Why not take a night-time tour to meet the rainforest's residents, most of which are nocturnal? Guides will take you out, armed with good shoes and torches, seeking pademelons, tree kangaroos, and ring-tailed possums. For many, a meeting of this sort with the nocturnal inhabitants of this Heritage Listed Wilderness will be the experience of a lifetime.

For others, a trip back to Port Douglas minus the torch and the sandshoes, to experience its nightlife and meet with its native inhabitants (many of whom are also nocturnal) could turn out to be just as memorable.

Here the salty smell of the sea meets the earthiness

of the rainforest... this band of sand divides them

Their ancient root systems and the murky mudcrab worlds below

Below: Mangroves at Cape Tribulation. Opposite: Lizard Island; crab feeding balls.

Cajun daintree

barramundi with kipfler potato salad, jelly coconut sambal and cumquat sauce

Serves 4

4 x 180g Barramundi
2 tbsps cajun spice
1 bunch fresh asparagus

kipfler potato salad

4 garlic cloves
olive oil & 2 egg yolks
1 tsp Dijon mustard
juice of 2 limes & 2 kaffir lime leaves, julienned
salt & pepper, to taste
1 cup grape seed oil
600g kipfler potatoes
1 red capsicum, finely chopped
1 spanish onion, thinly sliced

coconut sambal

200g jelly coconut, julienned
⅓ cup coconut cream
1 tsp fish sauce
½ red capsicum & ½ spanish onion, very finely chopped
⅓ cup chopped coriander
1 tbsp sweet chilli sauce
1 tbsp sesame oil

comquat sauce

1 kg cumquat
½ cup orange juice
2 cardamon pods
2 bay leaves
1 cinnamon quill
½ cup sugar
50g butter

To prepare the salad, place garlic on a baking tray and drizzle with olive oil and bake in a 180°C oven for 10 minutes or until soft. Place garlic, egg yolks, mustard, lime juice, kaffir lime leaves, salt and pepper in a food processor and process for 10 seconds. With the motor still running, add the oil in a thin stream. When the mixture starts to thicken you can add the oil faster. Continue to process until the mayonnaise is thick and creamy. Place potatoes in a pot of salted boiling water and cook until tender. Refresh in cold water. Slice potatoes thickly and then combine with capsicum, onion and lime mayonnaise.

To make the Sambal, combine coconut jelly, coconut cream, fish sauce, capsicum, onion, coriander, sweet chilli sauce and oil in a bowl and mix to combine.

To prepare the cumquat sauce, place all ingredients in a saucepan and bring to the boil. Reduce heat and simmer, uncovered, until liquid is reduced by half. Strain. Add butter just before serving.

Boil or steam asparagus for 2-3 minutes or until tender. Coat the Barramundi fillets with the cajun spice. Heat oil in frypan. Add fish and cook each side for approximately 2 minutes over a medium heat or until cooked.

To serve, place the kipfler potato salad on a serving plate with the asparagus then top with a barramundi fillet and the coconut sambal. Drizzle the cumquat sauce over the top.

Roasted chicken

breast on a honey sweet potato mash with wilted spinach and roasted garlic jus

Serves 4

ingredients
4 chicken breasts
salt & pepper, to taste
1 tbsp oil
3-4 chorizo sausages, cut into thin strips
250g spinach leaves

sweet potato mash
1kg sweet potato
2 tbsps butter
1 tbsp wholegrain mustard
1 tbsp honey
salt & cracked black pepper

roasted garlic jus
3-4 cloves garlic
1 tbsp olive oil
1 onion, roughly chopped
1 carrot roughly chopped
½ stick celery, roughly chopped
2 cups chicken stock
1 bay leaf
sprig of thyme
cracked black pepper

To prepare the jus, place garlic on a baking tray, drizzle with olive oil and bake in a 200°C oven for 10 minutes or until soft. Heat oil in frypan and sauté onion, carrot and celery until golden brown. Add the stock, bay leaf, thyme and pepper and cook until liquid is reduced by half. Add the garlic and simmer for a further 10 minutes. Remove from heat. Strain and set aside.

To make the mash, peel & wash sweet potato and roughly cut into chunks. Place into a pot of boiling water and cook until tender. Drain and place in a bowl together with butter, mustard and honey and mash. Season with salt and pepper. Keep warm.

Season chicken with salt and pepper. Heat oil in a hot frypan. Add chicken and sear for 30 seconds on both sides. Place breasts on a greased baking tray and bake in a preheated oven of 200°C for 15-20 minutes.

Heat oil in frypan. Add chorizo and cook over a medium heat until chorizo curls. Set aside and keep warm.

Place the spinach in a pot of salted boiling water and blanch for only a few seconds or until the spinach is soft.

To serve, place a portion of sweet potato mash onto a plate then top with spinach and chicken breast. Reheat the jus and pour a little over the chicken. Garnish with the chorizo.

Barramundi with asian

vegetables

Serves 4

ingredients

750g Barramundi fillets
salt and pepper
200g fresh thin rice noodles
½ cup castor sugar
1 cup soy sauce
½ cup rice vinegar (mitsukan)
1 tbsp sesame oil
1 cup eshallots, julienned
2 medium leeks (white part only), julienned
1 medium carrot, julienned
2 cloves garlic, finely chopped
1 tsp finely grated ginger
1 large red chilli, seeded & finely chopped
1 cup shitake mushrooms, sliced thinly
1 cup snow peas, julienned

Place noodles in a bowl. Pour boiling water over them to soften. Allow to stand for at least 5 minutes and then drain well.

Season Barramundi fillets with salt and pepper. Heat oil in a hot frypan. Add fillets and sear for 30 seconds on each side. Place fillets in a lightly oiled baking tray. Bake in a preheated 180°C oven for 5 minutes or until cooked.

Dissolve the sugar in the soy sauce and rice vinegar. Heat the oil in a wok or frypan. Add the eshallots, leeks, carrots, garlic, ginger, chilli, mushrooms and snow peas and stir-fry over a high heat for 1 minute. Add the soy mixture to the pan and cook for a further 1 minute.

To serve, place the noodles and stir-fried vegetables on a plate. Top with barramundi fillets and drizzle a little of the excess liquid over the top.

Barbeque kangaroo fillet

with a sweet corn relish, caramelised onion & honey served on a buckwheat pikelet

Serves 4

ingredients

500g kangaroo fillets
olive oil
4 sprigs rosemary, for garnish
1 tbsp honey

corn relish
¼ cup white sugar
¼ cup white wine vinegar
2 corn on the cob, kernels removed
1 small brown onion, finely chopped
1 medium red capsicum, finely chopped

buckwheat pikelet
1 cup buckwheat flour
1 tsp bicarbonate of soda (baking soda)
1 egg
¾ cup milk
2 tbsps oil

caramelised onion
1 tbsp butter
1 tbsp olive oil
3 brown onions, sliced
1 tbsp sugar

To make the relish, combine the sugar and vinegar in a saucepan and stir constantly over a low heat until the sugar dissolves. Add the corn, onion and capsicum and cook for approximately 20 minutes or until thick. Set aside and allow to cool.

To make the pikelets, sift flour and baking soda together into a mixing bowl. Add the egg and gradually stir in milk. Whisk until smooth. Heat oil in a non-stick frypan and drop a tablespoon of the mixture and cook on both sides until lightly browned. Keep the pikelets warm.

To make the caramelised onion, heat oil and butter in a frying pan. Add onions and cook over a medium heat for 10 minutes. Add sugar and cook a further 2 minutes or until the onions are brown and caramelised.

Trim kangaroo of all sinew (preferably have the butcher do this for you). Brush each fillet lightly with olive oil and place on a preheated barbecue or chargrill and cook over a high heat for approximately 1-2 minutes on all sides or until medium rare. Allow the fillets to rest for 1 minute before slicing.

To serve, place pikelets on serving plate with the caramelised onion. Top with the kangaroo and corn relish. Finally, drizzle a little bit of honey over the top. Garnish with rosemary.

Black sapote

mudcake

Serves 6-8

ingredients
150g chocolate buds
1-2 tbsps liqueur eg: Tia
Maria or Crème de Menthe
(optional)
250g butter
¼ cup milk
5 eggs, separated
¾ cup castor sugar
¼ cup self-raising flour
¼ cup hazelnut meal
1 medium black sapote,
finely chopped

chocolate glaze
125g dark chocolate, chopped
125g unsalted butter

Place the chocolate buds, liqueur, butter and milk in a saucepan over a low heat and stir until smooth. Set aside. Place egg yolks and sugar in a bowl and beat until light and creamy. Gradually fold the chocolate mixture, sifted flour, hazelnut meal and chopped sapote into the egg and sugar mixture. Place the egg whites in a separate bowl and beat until soft peaks form. Fold the egg whites through the chocolate mixture. Pour the mixture into a 20 cm (8 inch) round cake tin lined with non-stick baking paper. Preheat oven to 180°C. Bake for approximately 40 minutes. Turn onto a wire rack to cool.

To make the glaze, place the chocolate and butter in a saucepan and stir until smooth. Set aside and cool to room temperature.

To finish, spread cake with the glaze then refrigerate to set.

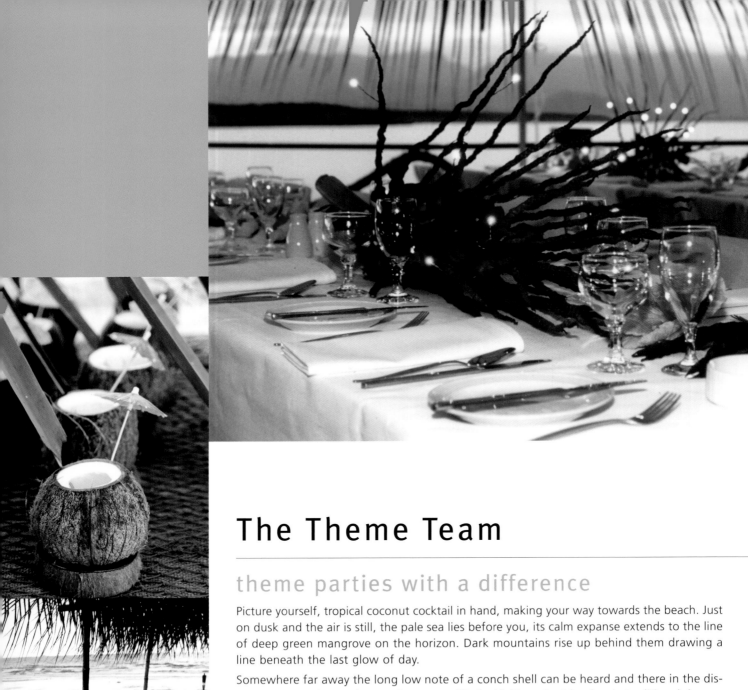

The Theme Team

theme parties with a difference

Picture yourself, tropical coconut cocktail in hand, making your way towards the beach. Just on dusk and the air is still, the pale sea lies before you, its calm expanse extends to the line of deep green mangrove on the horizon. Dark mountains rise up behind them drawing a line beneath the last glow of day.

Somewhere far away the long low note of a conch shell can be heard and there in the distance, you can just make out the canoes filled with Thursday Islanders in traditional dress… Soon, accompanied by torch bearers, you will be captivated by their performance of dance and music, leading you into your Coral Sea Dreaming theme night. Just one of a variety of The Theme Team's dream nights translated into reality for your convention or incentive tour.

restaurant index

Botanical Ark

4oo different species of tropical fruits & nuts!

Journey past the cane paddocks and into the back blocks of the Douglas Shire and you will find the most amazing variety of fruit to be found anywhere on earth. Over the past three decades, a few dedicated individuals have tirelessly searched the world's tropical rainforests and their efforts have resulted in the introduction into Australia of more than 400 different species of tropical fruits & nuts. Together with a band of enthusiastic backyard and commercial growers, they formed the Mossman branch of the Rare Fruits Council of Australia and have met regularly for the past 20 years to discuss, share and enjoy all they can about rare fruits. Some of these 'rare' fruits are now produced in abundance supplying not only Port Douglas but cities far to the south.

Local chefs have been keen to 'discover' these new fruits and if you are lucky enough you may enjoy them as part of some incredible new culinary creation. As the new fruits become more readily available they will continue to work their way into a cuisine which is both unique and refreshing. Restaurants often say they can create almost anything, given enough time and money, and that miracles take a little longer. Here in paradise, miracles are small red berries that grow on shrubs or small trees. Originally from Nigeria, these shrubs make even the most sour and acidic dishes taste deliciously sweet. Yes, miracles are available almost perennially in Port Douglas.

Some of these new fruits are so rare and difficult to grow that they are available only briefly, if at all, and it may be decades before they are relatively common. While Black Sapotes, Rambutans, Mangosteens, Durians, Mameys, Caimitos and Rollinias are now common, look out in the future for Itangas, Tauns, Isaus, Bukbuks, Pedalis, and Cupuacus. Never heard of these? Not to worry, rumour has it a new dictionary of tropical fruit names will be published some day. ALAN & SUSAN CARLE

Black Sapotes

Rambutans

Mangosteens

Durians

Mameys

Caimitos

Rollinias

Itangas

Tauns

Isaus

Bukbuks

Pedalis

Cupuacus

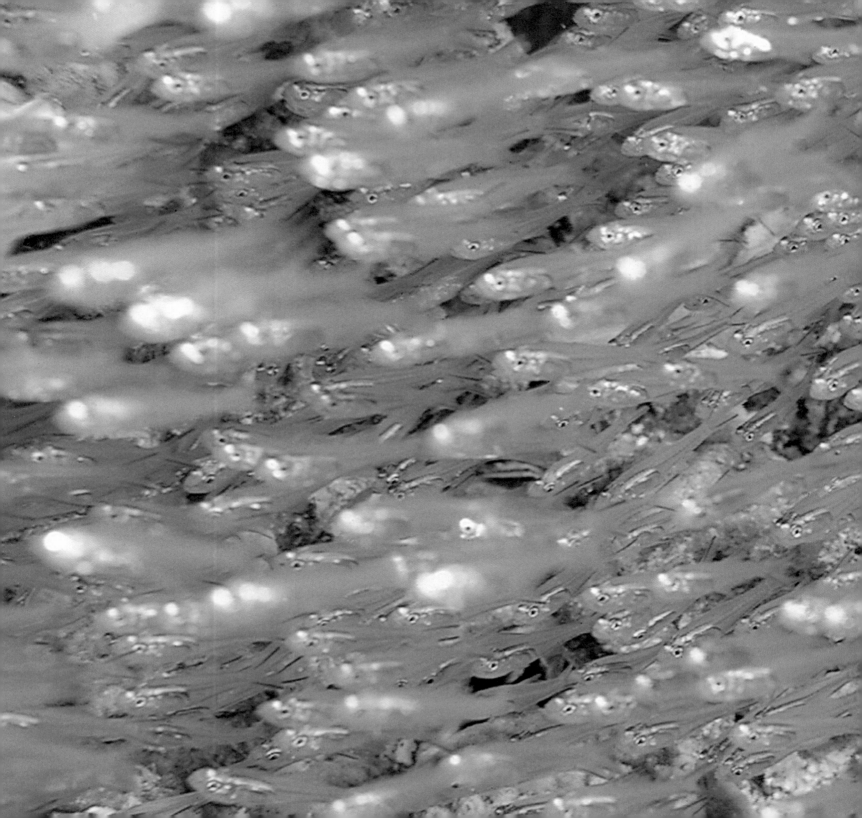